C000061827

BODY LANGUAGE READING:

The complete guide to reading the person in front of you and thus obtaining a psychological and negotiating advantage

Oliver Bennet

Table of Contents

© **Copyright 2020 Oliver Bennet - All rights reserved.**

The content contained within this book may not be reproduced, duplicated or transmitted without direct written permission from the author or the publisher.

Under no circumstances will any blame or legal responsibility be held against the publisher, or author, for any damages, reparation, or monetary loss due to the information contained within this book. Either directly or indirectly.

Legal Notice:

This book is copyright protected. This book is only for personal use. You cannot amend, distribute, sell, use, quote or paraphrase any part, or the content within this book, without the consent of the author or publisher.

Disclaimer Notice:

Please note the information contained within this document is for educational and entertainment purposes only. All effort has been executed to present accurate, up to date, and reliable, complete information. No warranties of any kind are declared or implied. Readers acknowledge that the author is not engaging in the rendering of legal, financial, medical or professional advice. The content within this book has been derived from various sources.

Please consult a licensed professional before attempting any techniques outlined in this book.

By reading this document, the reader agrees that under no circumstances is the author responsible for any losses, direct or indirect, which are incurred as a result of the use of information contained within this document, including, but not limited to, — errors, omissions, or inaccuracies.

Chapter 1: Facial Expressions

Wrinkles convey the intensity of emotions and the degree of originality of the emotion. In most cases, wrinkles convey hardship and suffering, as well as extreme anger. Wrinkles can also indicate one is always smiling, senile, or nasty.

Facial expressions and emotions are related. Facial expressions can create an emotional experience. Smiling tends to induce more pleasant moods while frowning induces negative moods. In this manner, facial expressions may cause emotion by generating physiological changes in the body. Through the self-perception process, people assume that they

must be sad or happy because they are smiling or frowning, and these cause emotions.

Other factors beyond facial expressions cause emotions. For instance, emotions are largely a function of the human system of beliefs and stored information. In other terms, you feel angry when you score less than average marks because the current system equates that to not being smart enough. And the stored information reminds you that you risk repeating the test or not securing a plum employment position, and this entire matter makes you feel hopeless, upset, and stressed.

There is a possibility that if the belief system did not deem less than average as a failure and the stored information shows a positive outlook for such a score, you will feel happy or excited.

Additionally, twitching your mouth randomly; either way indicates that one is deliberately not listening or degrading the importance of the message. The facial gesture is realized by closing the lips and randomly twitching the mouth to either the right or left akin to swirling the mouth with mouthwash. The facial expression is also to indicate outright disdain to the speaker or the message. The facial expression is considered rude to express disgust with the speaker or the message and should be avoided at all costs.

Where one shuts their lips tightly, it indicates that the individual is feeling angry but does not wish to show the anger. Shutting the lips tightly may also indicate that the person feels uneasy but struggles to concentrate at all costs. The source of the discomfort could be the immediate neighbors, the message, or the speaker. Through this gesture, the individual indicates he or she simply wants the speaker to conclude the speech because not all people are enjoying the message.

When one is angry or strongly disapproves of what the speaker says, the person will grimace. A grimace indicates that the person is feeling disgusted by what is being said. In movies or during live interviews, you probably so the interviewee grimaces when an issue or a person that the person feels is disgusting is stated. Showing a grimace indicates one harbors a strong dislike for the message or the speaker. A person that is feeling uncomfortable due to sitting on a hard chair, a poorly ventilated room, or sitting next to a hostile neighbor may also show a grimace, which is not necessarily related to the message.

If one is happy, then one is likely to have a less tense face and a smile. Positive news and positive emotions are manifested as a smile or a less tense facial look. On the other hand, if one is processing negative emotions, then the person's face is likely to be tensed up due to exerting pressure on the body muscles. A genuine smile like when one is happy is wider than an average curve and is temporary. A prolonged smile that is very wide suggests the individual is smirking at the message or the speaker. A prolonged smile may also suggest the individual is faking the emotion.

By the same measure, a frozen face may indicate intense fear. For instance, you have seen terrified faces when attending a health awareness forum on sexually transmitted diseases or some medical condition that terrified the audience. In this setting, the face of the audience will appear as if it has been paused. The eyes and the mouth may remain stationary as the speaker presents the scary aspects of the medical condition. It appears negative emotions may slow down the normal conscious and unconscious movement of the muscles of the face.

The appropriateness of facial expressions varies among subcultures of the same cultural group. Compared to the Japanese, Americans readily manifest anger, and this shows that individuals express emotion differentially across cultures.

If you are a teacher or trainer, then you encounter facial expressions from your students frequently. Assuming that you are a teacher, then you have noticed facial expressions indicating shock, uneasiness, and disapproval when you announce tests or indicate that the scores are out.

From these facial expressions, you will concur that the students feel uncomfortable, uncertain, and worried. The students will show lines of wrinkles, look down, eyes wide open and mouths agape when sudden and uncomfortable news is announced. Even though the students may indicate they are prepared for the test, their facial expressions suggest otherwise.

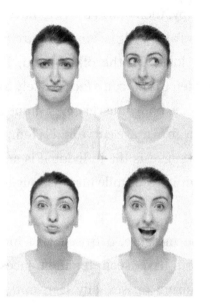

Like all forms of communication, effective reading of facial expressions will happen where the target person is unaware that you are reading even though they understand that their facial expressions are integral to the overall communication. In other words, when one becomes aware he or she is being studied, the person will act expectedly or simply freeze the expected reaction. It is akin to realizing that someone is feeling you.

Since the underlying emotion affects the facial expression that one shows. As indicated, the body language overrides verbal communication, which helps reveal the true status of an individual. One possible argument of the body language triumphing over verbal communication is that the body prioritizes its physiological needs over other needs. The physiological needs are critical to the survivability of an individual.

Over centuries the human body could have been programmed to increase survivability rate by prioritizing physiological needs. Body language largely indicates the physiological state of an individual, which is meant to help the individual and others respect the person's true physiological status.

Imagine what could happen where one is sickly, and it is worsening, but the person manages to manifest a convincing body language of happiness and enthusiasm. The outcome would be prioritizing the emotional needs of the individual over the physiological needs. Apart from laboratory tests and physical examination, it would be difficult for other people to realize that something is amiss and ask the individual to take rest.

Without illness, when one feels anxious about the audience, he or she manifests disharmony of the physiological status. There is a necessity to make the person and the audience aware that the individual is suffering and that they should be understanding of the individual.

Chapter 2: How to Tell If Someone Is Faking a Facial Expression

There are several reasons why people choose to hide their facial expressions. For some, it is a way suppressing their emotions towards a given matter. As much as their words portray a particular image in your brain, it is their wish that you do not get to see their actual emotions on the same subject. For example, you may be holding a conversation with a potential partner who likes you but they are afraid to let you know that – maybe because they are too shy or unwilling to be the first ones to reveal that. Because of their unwillingness to express their emotions, they could try to fake their facial expressions. In such a case, it is up to you to discover that on your own. You have to look closely at their faces as they speak to you to get their actual feelings.

Some people have just too much ego that they wouldn't allow their facial expressions to be shown. When a particular matter has hurt them and that they are undergoing immense pain inside, their big egos would not let them reveal such details. These are the kinds of people who suffer in silence which could lead to a harmful situation – suicide, for example.

There is also this category of people who hide their facial expressions, not because they want to do so, but because they just do not know how to solve negative emotions. As negativity builds up from the inside and starts to show in the face, they soon device ways to hide any form of negative expressions to lock you out from analyzing them. They want to look happy when in real sense they are sad. They want you to see that they are having a good time but in reality, there is a sickness or school fees issue that has been stressing them for months. We all know that negative emotions can lead to frowning on one's face, which essentially makes them not so approachable or appealing. Thus, in an attempt to retain their attractiveness, they conceal any form of negative facial expression which would have otherwise confronted them.

In other cases, some people may hide their facial expressions just to please. These are the people who believe in the

philosophy that what you do not know cannot hurt you. Their idea is that when they keep some information from you, you may still have a happy life. Thus, when they speak to you, they will struggle to build a certain kind of facial expression which conveys the message that all is well while in real sense that is further from the truth. Let's say one of your best friends gets bad news from the doctor that they have cancer and that they have only a few years with you. They love you so much and know how much such news could be devastating to you. To save you all the pain, they may choose to struggle with the pain on their own, believing that you will have a happy life if provided you do not know about it. Whenever they tell stories with you, they will do their best not to let you go inside. From their facial expressions, they will be smiling for you whereas only they know the agony they are experiencing. You have the responsibility of decoding this so that you get the message they are trying to lock inside.

5 Signs Someone Is Being Fake: How To Tell They Are Faking Facial Expressions

1. Taking deep breath

This is a technique that seems to be universal amongst all people who express untrue facial expressions. You will often see them appear unrelated and continuously breathe in and out heavily in their explanations over a matter you just asked. Because they know that for you to believe the facial expression they just wore to impress you, they have to appear calm. That is what the deep breathes are meant to do – take in more oxygen so that they can recollect their composure and be cool. If you are not keen enough on the breathing pattern, their faces may appear calm to you and succeed in the deception.

2. Putting up a fake smile

A smile never says that someone is happy at all times. Someone who smiles and has a bubbly look on their face can win hearts and affection. As a result, many assume that with just the right smile, they will hide their feelings like anger or sadness. But a fake smile will always be fake. It may convince some people at the first glance but a keen individual will soon realize this smile is fake. How well you know the individual could help you distinguish between the smile they just put up and their real happy smile. But even if you do not know them that well, their inability to sustain the smile will eventually prove it fake.

3. Trying not to supporting the head

There is something about 'cooked' facial expressions that makes the head heavy. People who understand the technique of hiding facial expressions know this. Thus, they always try to make sure that their head is held up high to deceive you better. When you are keen on them, there will be these occasions when they can no longer hold the head up and end up burying the face in their palms for some seconds before realizing that they may show you that they are lying. Careful analysis of the struggles not to support the head could reveal that they are faking their facial expression.

4. Struggling to relax the face

A relaxed face can easily build up a deceiving facial expression. For example, your son may have committed an offense in school and they come to report the matter to you, hoping to come out as victims. If your first glance on their faces shows them as being relaxed, you could be deceived and even get on the wrong side with the teachers. However, if you saw their faces were not relaxed even before they started the explanation, you can tell right away that there must be a problem somewhere. When you speak to someone and their face is relaxed at one time and at the other one it is not, that is a sign of a problem. Within a few minutes their face could be straight while at another it is steel and acting like a tough guy. This shows that they may have tried to relax it up to a certain point when they could do it no more. There is something here; take a deep look at their faces and you shall see it.

5. Silent lip movements

To be calm, some people speak to themselves. They may say something like "Calm down, you can do this. Just stay cool." If you are not careful, they may succeed in being calm and creating a falsified facial expression. Through a keen look at the lip movements, you may tell that they have more things that they are hiding under their facial expressions.

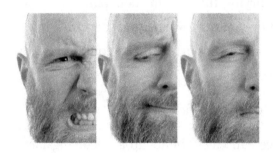

Chapter 3: Posture and Body Orientation

Posture and body orientation should be interpreted in the context of the entire body language to develop the full meaning and being communicated. Starting with an open posture, it is used to denote amicability and costiveness.

In this open position, the feet are placed openly, and the palms of the hands are facing outward. Individuals with open posture are deemed more persuasive compared to those with other stances.

To realize an open stance, one should stand upright or sit straight with the head upright and maintain the abdomen and chest bared. When the open posture is combined with an easy facial expression and good visual contact, it makes one look approachable and composed. Maintain the body facing forward toward the other person during a conversation.

There is also the closed posture where one crosses the arms across the chest or crosses the legs or sits in a facing a forward position as well as displaying the backs of the hands and closing the fists are indicative of a closed stance.

The closed posture gives the impression that one is bored, hostile, or detached. In this posture, one is acting cautious and appears ready to defend themselves against any accusation or threat.

The confident posture helps communicate that one is not feeling anxious, nervous, or stressed. The confident posture is attained by pulling oneself to full height, holding the head high, and keeping the gaze at eye level. Then bring your shoulders backward and keep the arms as well as legs to relax by the sides. The posture is likely to be used by speakers in a formal context such as when making a presentation, during cross-examination and project presentation.

Equally important, there is postural echoing and is used as a flirting technique by attracting someone in the Guardian. It is attained by observing and mimicking the style of the person and the pace of movement. When the individual leans against the wall, replicate the same.

By adjusting your postures against the others to attain a match, you are communicating that you are trying to flirt with the individual. The postural echoing can also be used as a prank game to someone you are familiar with and often engage in casual talk.

Maintaining a straight posture communicates confidence and formality. Part of the confidence of this posture is that it maximizes blood flow and exerts less pressure on the muscle and joints, enhancing the composure of an individual. The straight posture helps evoke desirable mood and emotion, which makes an individual feel energized and alert. A straight posture is a highly preferred informal conversation such as during meetings, presentations, or speech.

Correspondingly being in a slumped position and hunched back is a poor posture and makes one lazy, sad, or poor. A slumped position implies a strain to the body, making the individual feel less alert and casual about the ongoing conversation.

On the other hand, leaning forward and maintaining eye contact suggests that one is listening keenly. During a speech, if the audience leans forward in an upright position, it indicates that they are eager and receptive to the message.

Furthermore, if one slants one of the shoulders when participating in a conversation, it suggests that the individual is tired or unwell. Leaning on one side acutely while standing or sitting indicates that you are feeling exhausted or fed up with the conversation and are eagerly waiting for the end or a break.

Think of how you or others reacted when a class dragged on to almost break time. There is a high likelihood that the audience slanted one of their shoulders to left or right direction. In this state, the mind of the individual deviates to things that one will do next. In case of a tea break, the students' minds will deviate to what one will do during or after the tea break.

By the same measure standing on one foot indicates that one is feeling unease or tired. When one stands on one foot, it suggests that the person is trying to cope with discomfort. The source of uneasiness could be emotional or physiological.

For instance, you probably juggled your body from one foot to ease the need to go for a short call or pass wind. It is a way to disrupt the sustained concentration that may enhance the disturbing feeling.

If one cups their head or face with their hands and rests the head on the thighs, the individual feels ashamed or exhausted.

When the speaker mentions something that makes you feel embarrassed, you are likely to cup their face or head and rest the face on the thighs. It is a literal way of hiding from shame.

Children are likely to manifest this posture though while standing. When standing this posture may make one look like he or she is praying.

Additionally, if one holds their arms akimbo while standing, the individual shows a negative attitude or disapproval of the message. The posture is created by holding the waist with both hands while standing up straight and facing the target person. The hands should simultaneously grip on the flanks, the part near the kidneys. In most cases, the arms-akimbo posture is accompanied by disapproval or sarcastic face to denote attitude, disdain, or disapproval.

When one stretches both of their shoulders and arms and rests them on chairs on either side, then the individual is feeling tired and casual. The posture is akin to a static flap of wings where one stretches their shoulder and arms like wings and rests them on chairs on either side. It is one of the postures that loudly communicates that you are bored, feeling casual, and that you are not about the consequences of your action.

The posture is also invasive of the privacy and space of other individuals and may disrupt their concentration.

If one bends while touching both of their knees, the individual feels exhausted and less formal with the audience. The posture may also indicate extreme exhaustion and need to rest.

For instance, most soccer players bend without kneeling while holding both of their knees, indicating exhaustion. Since in this posture, one is facing down, it may be highly inappropriate in formal contexts and may make one appear queer.

When one leans their head and supports it with an open palm on the cheeks, it indicates that one is thinking deeply and probably feeling sad, sorrowful, or depressed.

The posture is also used when watching something with a high probability of negative outcomes such as a movie or a game. The posture helps one focus deep on the issue akin to meditating.

Through this posture, an individual tries to avoid distractions and think deeper on what is being presented.

If you watch European soccer, you will realize that coaches use this posture when trying to study the match, especially where their team is down. However, this posture should not be used in formal contexts as it suggests rudeness. The posture should be used among peers only.

Then there is the crossing of the legs from the thigh through the knee while seated on a chair, especially on a reclining chair. In this posture, one is communicating that he or she is feeling relaxed and less formal.

 In most cases, this posture is exhibited when one is at home watching a movie or in the office alone past working hours. If this posture is replicated in a formal context, then it suggests boredom or lack of concentration.

For the posture where one crosses the legs from the ankle to the soles of the feet while seated, it communicates that one is trying to focus in an informal context such as at home. For instance, if a wife or a child asks the father about something that he has to think through, then the individual is likely to exhibit this posture. If this posture is replicated in a formal context, then it suggests boredom or lack of concentration.

Chapter 4: Arms

A great deal of our emotions is expressed through our arms. Much of our productivity depends on the accuracy of our arms when completing tasks. The movements of the arms are quite obvious as they are used as a complement to verbal expression. The arms are able to extend towards an individual, either in a threat or in a very friendly manner when they moved either quickly or directly.

However, they may give much comfort when they are curved and moving more slowly. The arms can also extend laterally. The arms can also be used to show aggression and some sort of confidence. The arms can also be used in shaping, as they are waved out to the world to pass out certain information. These parts of the body can also be used as certain adjuncts to the words that we speak, as they are used to show how something is either big or small. When we are either confident or excited, the arms can be used to pass the message. We may wave them out to show our displeasure or excitement. Each time we lose our confidence, our shaping will be next to our bodies and a bit smaller. The waving of the arms requires control, and an individual who claps or beats their hands-on certain things may be considered to be showing some sort of clumsiness.

Raising the arms is also a way of saying something. When the arms are raised immediately, it shows that the speaker is dismissing certain things. When it is done with both arms, it even exaggerates the whole matter. A typical two arms that are raised shows a sign of giving up and frustration. It can also be used as a sign of showing surrender, like in the case of someone who is cornered in a fixed situation. When the arms are raised and coupled with a shrug, it can show some confusion.

It is also very important to note that the arms can be used as weapon. The arms can symbolize the spears and clubs as they strike out some  foes in the imaginary spaces. The arms can also be very defensive, at times, sweeping and blocking away attacks from enemies. This is most common in the martial arts spaces.

The arms that are crossed can also be used to show some communication. Arms can be used as the main entrant to the body of a human being. When the arms are crossed, they tend to create a closed and defensive shield, and barring the outside world. The shields are used to playing two major roles; one is to stop all the incoming attacks, while the other role is to show that a person is hiding and does not want to be seen. The crossed arms may also show some sort of anxiety that can be fueled either in the absence of trust in the other person or even an internal discomfort. It can also be used to show a vulnerability that can be deeply anchored in childhood traumas.

The extent to which an arm is closed how a person might also be firmly closed. In most cases, this could vary from just a light cross of hands to folded arms or the ones that are wrapped around someone. A tightly closed arm with the hands formed as fits is one extreme version that can show someone is in a new hostility status. If the legs are also crossed, then much is added to the signal. The hands in the crossed arms may also be used to hold the individual in a kind of self-hug, for instance, grabbing the upper arms in a folded arms position or even wrapped around the torso, while holding the sides. If by any chance, the thumbs are up, then this could be a full indication that the person is in full agreement or approval of what is being said.

Arms that are crossed, particularly when holding each other can indicate that the person is trying as much as possible to remain calm and still. It can also be a way of suppressing any other signals that could have been passed out. In other instances, it can also be used to show a repressed kind of anger. There are certain cultures where this kind of arm signal is used to show that the person is holding themselves still so that they can pay much attention to the person they are talking with, and therefore, comes out as a great compliment. Crossed arms, particularly those in a folded position can just be used that the person is feeling very comfortable, particularly if there is very little tension somewhere in the body. When a person is comfortable, it becomes evident that they are fearless, and that mostly happen when someone is with friends. Arms that are folded with just a little more tension may show that the person is in a judgmental kind of situation.

When the arms are not closed, they tend to expose the torso and other parts of the body, making them appear so vulnerable. Apart from signifies comfort, it also shows some signs of trust. It can also be the position of power that dares the other person to go ahead and attack while knowing that the other person might not dare. Crossed arms are one of the most obvious arm signals. When it is done in front of a huge number of people, there are higher chances for them to feel rejected and later on respond. It is also very important to note that all crossed arms are defensive, like in the case of a person who is just relaxed.

The crossed arms signals are also used when the person feels some cold and want to get warmth by tucking the arms to keep them warm. There is a very common method that salespeople do to their customers. They ask them to hold something for them or give them their hand. This is a way of breaking the closed arm position of the customers in a polite manner.

Reaching forward to the other individual can be scary as it poses some dangers such as an attack. A sudden forward thrust can also be a very aggressive signal, particularly is the hand is shaped or pointing out just like a fist. The arms can also be pulled back to pass a message. When these body parts have been pulled back or in a thrust forward kind of position, they become in great danger or attack. When one feels defensive, they may opt to pull back their arms out of any impending danger.

When the arms are held behind, they are hidden from a place where people can easily see them. When this happens, it may be because it has a hidden intention or is trying to conceal something. All in all, it can be a very threatening signal. Arms in the backside expose the torso, which, in return, creates some sort of vulnerability. It can either signal comfort or submission. The main reason for comfort could be that the person is in the company of friends or feels so powerful and confident that others can't attack them.

Chapter 5:   Hand and Leg

How to Read Hand Gestures

Hand gesturing is a natural part of us. We use it without even thinking twice about it, sometimes a bit too much when excited or extremely emotional. Hand gestures are just as much a part of our communication process as our words.

When used correctly, gesturing makes people notice what you are trying to say, especially when you accompany those gestures correctly with the words you are trying to emphasize. Hand gestures reveal hidden clues about what a person may be thinking or feeling.

Here is how to decipher some of the most commonly used hand gestures:

- Brow Rubbing: This gesture indicates that a person could be worried or doubtful.

- Scratching the Head: Scratching the head could indicate a person who is in deep thought or trying to solve a problem; depending on the context, it could also indicate confusion.

- Running Fingers through Hair: Closely related to head scratching, this is often an indication that a person feels uncertain or unsure or trying to think of something.

- Eye Rubbing: An indication that a person is feeling fatigued.

- Index Finger on Temple: This gesture indicates that a person could be thinking of something. Sometimes, it is also an indication of a person in critical thoughts.

- Nose Touching: Generally associated with being an indication that a person is lying. If casually done, it could be an indication that the person feels pressured about something.

- Covering of the Mouth: If this gesture appears when a person is listening to someone else, it is an indication that the listener does not necessarily believe the speaker. If someone does this while talking, it could be an indication of dishonesty. Sometimes, it is also an indication that a person is thinking hard about something

- Lip Holding: This is often an indication that a person is feeling greedy.

- Putting Fingers in the Mouth: This gesture indicate that a person may need further reassurance before making a decision.

- Stroking of the Chin: This gesture normally indicates that a person is thinking.

- Ear Rubbing: Rubbing behind the ear is an indication that a person is afraid of being misunderstood or afraid of not understanding.

- Earlobe Touching: Touching the earlobe is an indication that a person is looking for comfort.

- Open Palms or Outstretched Arms: An indication of openness, trustworthiness, and acceptance.

- Palms Down: Palms down normally indicates confidence and is sometimes a sign of rigidness and a sense of authority.

- Hands behind the Back: Hand behind the back is an indication of confidence—most commonly used by men.

- Finger Pointing: This gesture is an indication that a person is feeling authoritative. At other time, it serves as an indication of aggressive or angry emotions.

How to Read Leg Movements

Who would have thought the position of a person's legs could reveal so much about what a person is thinking and feeling. Most of the time, we focus so much on what the upper body language of a person communicates that we forget about the legs and the story they tell.

Here are some hidden messages that a person could reveal with his or her leg movements:

- Sitting Down, Legs Slightly Apart: This indicates that the person is feeling both relaxed and comfortable.

- Legs Crossed While Standing: This indicates that the person could be feeling shy. We can consider it a submissive stance or indicate that a person does not feel entirely comfortable in specific surroundings or the company.

- Legs Crossed and Relaxed While Sitting: A very common gesture in many Asian and European cultures—70% of people generally cross their left leg over their right. However, when accompanied with arms crossed over the chest, this gesture can indicate an emotionally withdrawn or closed off person.

- Sitting Down, Ankles Crossed: An indication that the person is feeling fairly relaxed. If accompanied by clenched hands, this could indicate that the person is feeling rigid or tense, or a signal of self-restraint.

- Sitting Down, Ankles Crossed, and Tucked under Chair: This gesture could indicate a person trying to hide his or her feelings of anxiety.

- Sitting Down, Knees Pointed: If the person's knees are pointing towards you, it is an indication that the person finds you interesting or that he or she likes you. If the knees point away from you, it is an indication of disinterest.

- Standing, Leg Bouncing/Foot Tapping: This gesture indicates that that the person could be feeling impatient.

- Sitting, Leg Bouncing: If a person is moving his or her legs up and down while sitting, it is an indication of impatience. Sometimes, depending on the context, the person could be bouncing his or her leg or tapping the foot when either relaxed or enjoying the environment (for example, if music is playing in the background).

- Standing Parallel, Feet Close Together: This is an indication that a person is displaying a neutral attitude—often considered a more formal standing position.

- Standing, Legs Apart: This is predominantly common among men. It indicates a person is firm and standing his ground. Often seen when a person is trying to display a sense of dominance.

- Sitting, Figure Four Crossed Leg - If accompanied by both hands clamped down on the crossed leg, it is an indication that the person could be someone who has a competitive, stubborn, or tough nature.

Chapter 6:   Touch and Eye Contact

Touch

We engage in touching regularly, and it includes patting someone on

the back or granting someone a hug to indicate we care. We commonly shake hands as greetings or assign to signal shared understanding. Touch, as a form of communication, is called haptics. For children, touch is a crucial aspect of their development. Children who do not get adequate touch have developmental issues. Touch helps babies cope with stress. At infancy, touch is the first sense that an infant respond to.

Functional Touch

In the workplace, touch is among the most effective means of communication, but it is necessary to adhere to etiquette's common rules. For instance, a handshake is a form of touch used in the professional environment and can convey the relationship between two people. Pay attention to the nonverbal cues you are sending next time you shake someone's hand.

Overall, one should always convey confidence when shaking another person's hand, but you should avoid being overly-confident. Praise and encouragement are communicated by a pat on the back or a hand on the shoulder. One should remember that all people do not share the same comfort levels when using touch as nonverbal communication.

For instance, an innocent touch can make another person feel uneasy, and for this reason, applying touch requires reading the body language and responding accordingly.

Additionally, touch can become complicated at the workplace when touch is between a boss and a subordinate. Standard practice is that those in power are not allowed to touch subordinates rather than the other way around. For this reason, you should examine your motives for even the most trivial touches and resolve to enhance your communication techniques with your juniors. A standard measure is that it is better to fail on the side of caution. Functional touch includes being physically examined by a doctor and being touched as a form of professional massage.

Social Touch

Most forms of communication require some kind of touch. A handshake is a primary touch in social touches. Handshakes vary from culture to culture. It is socially polite and one is allowed to shake another person's hand during an introduction in the United States. In some countries, kissing on the cheek is the norm. In the same interactions, men will allow a male stranger to touch them on their shoulders and arms, whereas women feel comfortable being touched by a female stranger only on the arms. Men are likely to enjoy touch from a female stranger while women tend to feel uncomfortable with a male stranger.

Equally important, men and women process touch differently, which can create confusing and awkward situations. In most contexts, it might help unnecessary physical contact in social settings, especially those of the opposite sex. One should try to follow societal norms and to take cues from those around you. For instance, while you stand close to a stranger on an elevator, it is not acceptable to engage in any unnecessary physical contact.

Friendship Touch

The types of touches allowed between friends vary depending on contexts. For instance, women are more receptive, touching female friends compared to their male counterparts. The touches between female friends are more affectionate and often in the form of a hug, whereas men prefer to shake hands and pat each other on the back. Within family members, women touch each more other compared to men.

Additionally, same-sex family members are more likely to touch than family members of the opposite sex. Displays of affection between friends are critical in expressing support and encouragement, even if you are not a touchy-feely person. One should be willing to get out of their comfort zone and offer their friend a hug when they are going through a difficult time. Helping others enliven their mood is likely to uplift your mood as well.

Eye Contact

Reading eye contact is important in understanding an individual's true status, even where verbal communication seeks to hide it. As advised, body language should be read as a group. We will focus on individual aspects of body language and make the reader understand how to read that particular type of body language.

Starting with pupils, the pupil dilates when one is interested in the person they are talking to or the object we are looking at. The pupils will contract when one is transiting from one topic to another. We have no control over the working of pupils. When one is speaking about a less interesting topic, the pupils will contract.

Effective eye contact is critical when communicating with a person. Eye contact implies that one looks, but does not stare. Persistent eye contact will make the recipient feel intimidated or judged. In Western cultures, regular eye contact is desired, but it should not be overly persistent. If one offers constant eye contact, then it is seen as an attempt to intimidate or judge, which makes the recipient of the eye contact uncomfortable.

Some studies suggest most children fall victim to attacks by pet dogs if their eye contact is constantly regular as that causes the dog to feel threatened and defensive. Initiating an overly persistent eye contact is a sign of an individual's over-awareness of the emitting messages. Lying can be detected by the individual avoiding eye contact.

Evasive Eye Contact

Having evasive eye contact is a mark of discomfort. We avoid looking at a person if we feel ashamed to be communicating with them. When we feel dishonest about trying to deceive people, we avoid looking at them. While it is okay to blink or drop eye contact temporarily, people who consistently shun making eye contact are likely to be feeling uneasy with the message or the person they are communicating with. For emphasis, staring at someone will make them drop eye contact due to feeling intimidated. Evasive eye contact happens where one deliberately avoids making eye contact.

Crying

Human beings cry due to feeling uncontrollable pain or in an attempt to attract sympathy from others. Crying is considered as an intense emotion associated with grief or sadness though it can also denote extreme happiness known as tears of joy. When an individual forces tears to deceive others, it is known as crocodile tears, which imply faking tears to deceive others. If one cries, then the individual is likely experiencing intense negative emotion.

Blinking

In most cases, blinking is automatic, and our emotions and feelings directed towards the person we are speaking to can cause us to alter our rate of blinking subconsciously. If the average rate of blinking is six to 10 times per minute, then it is a strong indicator that an individual is drawn to the person they are speaking to, and it is indicative of flirting. In normal contexts, men and women blink at the same rate as each other.

Winking

In Western culture, winking is considered a form of flirting that should be done to people we are in good terms with. There are cross-cultural variations on the issue of winking with Asian cultures frowning on winking as a form of facial expression.

Eye Direction

The direction of the eyes tells us about how an individual is feeling. When someone is thinking, they tend to look to their left when they are recalling or reminiscing. An individual who is thinking tends to look to their right when eliciting creative thoughts. It can be interpreted as an indicative sign of someone trying to be deceitful in some situations such as creating a version of events. For left-handed people, the eye directions will be reversed.

Additionally, when one is interested in what you are saying, he or she will often make eye contact. Some studies found that when people are engaged in an interesting conversation, their eyes focus on the face of their partner, about 80% of the time but not wholly on the eyes. Rather, the eye contact on the other person's eyes is for the duration of two to three minutes, then move down to the lips or nose then back up to the eyes. For a brief moment, the person initiating eye contact will look down then back up to the eyes. Looking up and to the right demonstrates dismissal and boredom. Dilation of the pupil may indicate someone is interested or that the room is brighter.

In some instances, sustained eye contact may signal you want to speak to the person or are interested in the person sexually. At one point, you have noticed a hard stare from a man towards a particular woman to the point the woman notices and asks the man what is that all about. In this case, eye contact is not being used to intimidate, but to single out the targeted person. You probably have seen a woman ask why that man is staring at me, then she proceeds to mind her own business, but on taking another look in the direction of the man, the stare is still there. In this manner, eye contact is used to single out an individual and make them aware that one is having sexual feelings towards the person.

However, people are aware of the impact of body language and will seek to portray the expected body language. For instance, an individual who is lying is likely to make deliberate eye contact frequently to sound believable. At one point, you knew you were lying but went ahead to make eye contact. You probably have watched movies where one of the spouses is lying but makes believable eye contact with others. The reason for this faked body language is because the person is aware of the link between making eye contact and speaking the truth.

Like verbal language, body language, and in particular, eye contact can be highly contextual. For instance, an individual may wink to indicate he or she agrees with the quality of the product being presented or that he or she agrees with the plan. Eye contact in these settings can be used as a coded language for a group of people. One of your classmates may have used a wink to indicate that the teacher is coming or to indicate that the secret you have been guarding is now out.

Chapter 7:   Use of Space

Beyond just considering how someone holds themselves in general, you must also look at how the individual wants to interact with the space around them. You can typically break down space around someone into several different categories. You can look at it in terms of horizontal and vertical space, and we will be considering both. Ultimately, people will naturally place themselves within different areas within the space around them, and you can usually figure out a lot about what is going on in their brains. You may realize that they seem quite confident in what they are doing—they know that they are making a decision to stand in the way that is going to help them, for example, or keeping the right distance to create the right impression.

There are two ways to look at this—horizontal proxemics will refer to how far away someone is willing to hold themselves from you. This can vary greatly from person to person and can shift depending upon what someone is comfortable with. On the other hand, there is the use of vertical proxemics. This refers to how high or low someone places themselves concerning those around them. Some people will naturally be higher than others just due to their natural heights, but even someone that is naturally quite short can make great use of vertical proxemics quite simply.

Vertical Proxemics

Vertical proxemics refers to the difference in height between two people and how the individuals will interact with height in general to show body language or to convey something. Generally speaking, people, like most other animals, tend to relate bigger or taller, with better and more dominant. While we as a species do not only follow the biggest men around, we still make great use of this use of space around us. Some people will naturally carry themselves highly—they will look at the world around them in a way that reflects this. Others will naturally try to shrink inwards and make themselves smaller.

In general, however, you can make use of this regardless of the height. Even if you are short and wanting to display dominance, all you have to do is create the illusion that you are taller and, therefore, more dominant. You can do this with very simple tricks—you could, for example, try standing in a way that tilts your chin up and back so you are looking down your nose at the other person. Instead of being seen as submissive because you are smaller, you have turned things around and you can position yourself in just the right way that they have no choice but to accept that dominance that you are asserting. All you had to do was tilt your head a little bit.

Of course, this can work the other way, too. When people are not very confident, they tend to tuck their chin inwards. This forces them to look in an upward direction to make eye contact. When you do this with someone else, you are naturally submitting to them in a sense—you are telling them that they get to dominate and control that setting in some way, shape, or form, and you are granting that control to them.

You see this a lot in flirting as well—women will usually look up through their eyelashes at the men that they are attracted to, while men will typically hold their heads up high when they are interacting with other women that they find attractive. This is a natural way that you can see this sort of dynamic play out. You have the man who is showing dominance and the woman who is naturally submitting to the man to some degree, showing that she is willing and ready to accept the man's dominance because she is interested in him.

You can see this in other contexts as well. Suppose you were to interact with a child, for example. In that case, you may find that you naturally get down on one knee when you want to have a heart to heart conversation with them—you do this because it allows you to place yourself not above, nor below the child—rather, you are facing the child directly. You are putting yourself on equal footing with the child to get your point across and this will help the child then understand the message better. This is commonly used in schools to help the students learn what they are learning from teachers—when teachers get down to their students' levels, the children tend to be more receptive to the information at hand in general, and that is quite powerful and compelling.

Horizontal Proxemics

However, when you want to look at horizontal proxemics, you are going to be considering just how far away you position yourself from other people. Generally speaking, this indicates the intimacy between people—when two people have a closer relationship with each other, they will usually find that they gravitate closer to each other. They will naturally attempt to position themselves so they can get closer just due to being in that particular relationship status.

For example, think about the last time you saw a married couple walking around together—you may notice that they do not seem to have any physical boundaries. They are entirely comfortable working incredibly closely with each other because they trust each other. They may even end up standing while touching each other closely because they do not mind—they are totally happy being within each other's bubbles.

When you compare that to the way that strangers will keep themselves naturally spaced out, you will see a huge difference. Strangers will usually attempt to resist having to get that close to other people—they do not want to feel like they have to sort of infringe upon each other's bubbles. If they do have to do so for any reason, they will usually do so without acknowledgment.

Ultimately, the horizontal distance that you keep from other people can primarily be broken down into four distinct distances: The intimate distance, the personal distance, the social distance, and the public distance. These become those bubbles that you want to protect and defend from being infringed upon when interacting with other people. Let's look at each one of these distances:

Intimate Distance

This particular distance is reserved for those that you are the closest to, as you would probably assume. This is getting very close and personal to someone else—you are generally within a foot or two of their general person, or you could even be touching them actively. This particular distance is only for those that are allowed to infringe so much upon you—you may allow for people such as your young children or your spouse to enter this space around you. These are people that are naturally going to be more intimate with you in general. You and your intimate partners will most likely be touching each other to some degree or another, and when you have young children, you know that they are all about being touched, held, and cuddled. Young infants need to be cuddled close to be able to nurse or to be bottle-fed, and even as they do get older, they want that sort of natural interaction between themselves and those around them. They crave that intimacy and it is a need for them, so babies typically get a pass to this entire system.

Personal Distance

This next distance is reserved for family and friends. Generally speaking, the closer that you get to the other person, the closer your relationship is with that person. Those that are the closest to you, such as parents, older children, and best friends may be allowed to get closer to you within this zone—they are allowed to approach more or less to that intimate zone level. However, those that are not as close to you, such as those that you do not know very well or that family member you have only met at family reunions but never even spoken to otherwise, will typically be held further away. This distance is generally anywhere from about 1.5 to 4 feet around your general person.

Within this distance, you are close enough that you can interact closely with someone else—you could potentially hug or shake hands. You are close enough that you do not have to talk very loudly, nor do you have to do very much to interact further. You are generally deemed, at the very least, some sort of friend at this stage, or perhaps an acquaintance for those on the outermost rings of this radius.

Social Distance

This distance is for people that you are actively interacting with but may not know very well, or at all. Generally speaking, those within your social distance are those you can interact with to some degree. It may be that person who just said hi to you to be polite, or it could be the person you are asking for help from at the grocery store. When you see this sort of interaction with other people, you can generally assume that the other person is not feeling very close to the other person and they do not care to stand that close to each other. They may not know each other, not like each other, or not trust each other, and ultimately, that will be up to some degree of interpretation.

Most often, this distance ranges between 4 and 12 feet—you may find that you are comfortable allowing some people closer when there is some barrier between you.

Public Distance

Finally, the public distance is a distance that is typically considered used for public speaking. When you are using this distance in any context, you are trying to ensure that you interact with other people in a crowd without singling anyone out or leaving anyone else out. This is the distance that you would take to be able to do just that—it is what changes a casual conversation into a more intimate interaction between yourself and someone else.

This distance is generally considered to be anything beyond roughly 12 feet and it is no longer held hostage by the fact that people used not to be able to yell very far. You now have access to speakers, microphones, and even large screens that can stream you acting or talking in real-time—this can be used so you can expand upon that public distance quite greatly, which is something that many people do these days. Just look at modern concerts—stadiums are huge to accommodate everything and everyone who wants to go and see the concert. This is accommodated through the use of a screen that will broadcast the feed for everyone else to see. Then, everyone can see, even if they are sitting too far away, to hear someone if they did not have that microphone or that camera in the first place.

Chapter 8: Breathing

There are different ways you can read someone's body language. It can be read by their leg and arm movements, facial expressions, eye contact, or smiles. Do you realize that how a person breathes has meaning, too?

Emotions and how you breathe are connected. You could read a person's feelings by watching the way they breathe. If emotions change, how they breathe might be affected. See if you can notice breathing patterns in your family, friends, coworkers, or significant other. They may not tell you exactly how they are feeling and it might depend on certain situations.

·   Deep breathing might indicate excitement, attraction, anger, fear, or love

Deep breathing is the easiest pattern to notice. If somebody suddenly starts to hold their breath, they might be feeling a little scared. If someone takes a deep breath and then shouts, they could be angry. Excited people, are experiencing shock, or are surprised might suck in a deep breath. They might also take in a deep breath and hold it for a few seconds. If their eyes start to glow this might indicate that they are surprised or excited. A person might start to breathe deeply if they feel an attraction toward another person. You may notice someone take a deep breath in, suck in their stomach and push their chest out to impress somebody they are attracted to.

- Sighing might signal hopelessness, sadness, or relief

When you sigh, you are letting out a deep, long breath that you can hear. Somebody might sigh if they are feeling relieved after a struggle has passed. They are thankful that their struggle is over. A sign might show sadness or hopelessness like somebody who is waiting for a date to show up. It could also show tiredness and disappointment.

- Rapid, heavy breathing might show fear and tiredness

You may have just seen a person rob a place and the police are chasing them. You notice they are breathing very rapidly. This is because their lungs need more oxygen since they exert a lot of energy. After all, they are running. Their bodies feel tired and their lungs are trying their best to keep up. We feel the same effects when we feel scared. This will happen when we experience fear; our lungs need more oxygen, so we begin to breathe faster. You will easily see when somebody has been scared or running by noticing the way they are breathing.

Another interesting fact about breath is that smells can influence breath. Any odors that are tied to emotions can change a person's respiration rate. Several studies have shown that the body will respond to bad and good smells by breathing differently. If you were to smell something rotten, you would end up breathing in a shallow and rapid manner. But, if, instead, you smelled baking bread and roses, your breath would be slow and long. The really exciting part of this is that the breathing rate will change before the brain has ever been able to conscious register if the smell is good or bad.

According to Scientific American, the emotions that we have with smells and scents are extremely associative. We started learning about these different smells in the womb, and then during our lives, our brains learn to refine our views of emotional rewards, pleasures, and threats that are contained within a certain odor. If a person breathes deeply, they feel that something is safe, and it creates a pleasurable emotional state. This means if you notice a person's breathing rate suddenly change, let your sense of smell catch up first. It could be that they have gotten a whiff of something they either like or dislike.

The interesting thing is that while we can learn how people feel based on how they are breathing, the way a person breathes can also affect their emotions. In a 2006 study, published in Behavior Response & Therapy, they discovered that undergraduates who practiced slow-breathing exercises for 15 minutes had a more positive and balanced emotional response afterward than the group who were faced with 15 minutes of unfocused worrying and attention.

And it doesn't even have to do with just being calm. In a study by the French scientist Pierre Phillipot, he asked some participants to identify the pattern of breath connected with certain emotions such as sadness and joy. They then asked a separate group of people to breathe in a certain manner and probed their feelings. The results they got were excellent. If the subjects were told to live in a particular way, even if they were unaware of it, they said that they felt the feeling associated emotion, apparently, out of nowhere.

This is something that you can't readily do, but it is still impressive.

A new idea that is being studied about emotions and breath is that what you exhale also plays a role in emotional response. The chemically analyzed exhales were able to figure out how the person felts. In an article from Science News, the chemical makeup of the air within a soccer stadium varies when people begin cheering and the same is true

in movie theaters. They studied 9500 people as they watched 16 different films that ranged from rom-coms to horrors, and then they checked the air composition of the room to see if it changed during certain scenes that were rather emotional in one way or the other.

The crazy thing is that it did. In suspenseful moments, more CO_2 and isoprenes are in the air, which are chemicals associated with the tensing of muscles. Every type of emotion came with its chemical makeup.

Chapter 9: Laughter

The laughter is a response biologically produced by the body in response to certain stimuli. The smile is considered a soft and silent form of laughter. There are currently various interpretations about its nature.

It is popularly considered a response to moments or situations of humor, as an external expression of fun, and related to joy and happiness. However, according to numerous studies, such as Robert Provine, laughter is motivated by a comic stimulus in a minority of everyday cases. It usually appears, more or less simulated, as an emotional complement to verbal messages, and in situations of stress or playful behaviors such as tickling.

Some medical theories attribute beneficial effects on health and well-being to laughter, since it releases endorphins.

Forms of Laughter

Depending on the force with which it occurs, laughter can vary in its duration and tone and characteristics. Thus, we use different words to describe what we consider different types of laughter: click, laugh, laugh, giggle, contemptuous, desperate, nervous, equivocal laughter. Other types: caquino, jingle, evil laugh, hypoid.

Among the emotional cues, the smile is the most contagious of all, and smiling encourages positive feelings. Like the laugh itself, the smile is innate, and deaf and blind children smile. It usually appears at six weeks of life and is the first language of the human being. Initially it is a physical behavior, and gradually evolves into an emotional action. Self-induction of the gesture of smiling can improve our mood. Another property is to induce an increase in NK cells' activity and thus improve our immune status.

Some studies show that laughter varies by gender: women tend to laugh in a more singing way, while men tend to laugh snorting or growling.

Physiology of Laughter

It occurs when a stimulus - internal or external - is processed in primary, secondary and multimodal association areas of the central nervous system. The processing of emotions is carried out in the limbic system, which is probably responsible for the potential motors that characterize laughter, including facial expression and the muscles' movements that control ventilation and phonation. Once the stimulus has been processed and the aforementioned automatic motor acts, a generalized autonomous activation is carried out, which has an exit through several routes, among which are the Hypothalamus-pituitary axis and the autonomic nervous system. All these components make up the emotion. This process involves, when it comes to joy, the motor act called laughter.

There are two structures of the limbic system involved in the production of laughter: the amygdala and the hippocampus.

Some Studies

Laughter can be induced by stimulating the subthalamic nucleus, and it has been proven in patients with Parkinson's disease. A recent work by Itzhak Fried et al., Of the University of California, has allowed us to locate an area of the brain called a supplementary motor area. When stimulated using electrodes, it produces the smile and, with a more intense stimulation, laughing out loud. The supplementary motor area is an area very close to the language area. This mechanism was discovered accidentally while treating a young woman with epilepsy.

Experiments have been conducted to determine exactly in which area the sense of humor resides. In a study, presented in 2000 by scientists at the University of Rochester, volunteers underwent functional magnetic resonance while asking them various questions. They concluded that this characteristic resided in a small region of the frontal lobe. However, another London team performed the same test on individuals who were told jokes. The results were that the brain area that was activated was the ventral prefrontal cortex and other regions involved in the language process when the joke's grace resided in a pun.

Robert Provine: Laughter as Communication

Popularly, laughter and smile are associated with happiness and good humor; however they are not reliable measures of mood. According to recent studies, laughter is a communication mechanism. It follows that the triggering factor of laughter is not happiness or joy in themselves, but the fact that there is at least one other person who can receive the message, in the form of playful nonsense. It has been proven that the relationship between laughter in society and laughter in solitude is 30 to 1. We need more people, and that they can laugh, to laugh.

Field Study

Provine sought to adopt a "naturalistic and descriptive tactic" to reveal the subconscious triggers and instinctive roots of laughter. He initially observed subjects in his laboratory, but found that laughter was too fragile, illusory and variable under direct scrutiny. Therefore, he decided to keep the appearance of natural and spontaneous laughter in daily life. He began to listen and secretly record the conversational laugh (the one that typically follows the conversation speech a second later), documenting 1200 episodes. He later studied the patterns of who laughed and when, to analyze their qualities. He concluded that for laughter to occur, more than one person is necessary, the minimum element being a dyad, a speaker and a listener (except in the case of a spectator laughing aloud watching television, for example). Laughter tended to follow a natural conversational rhythm, splashing the speech after complete statements, and especially after changes in volume or intonation. The most interesting thing was that less than a quarter of the previous comments were humorous. Provine suggests that laughter synchronizes the speaker and the listener's brains, in such a way that it serves as a signal for the receptive areas of language, perhaps switching the activation between competitive brain structures of cognition and emotion.

The observations of interpretation students laughing at the right time led him to conclude that laughter is under a relatively weak conscious control, and that the most natural-looking laughter is caused by subconscious mechanisms, which explains why method acting can lead to the reproduction of emotions more effectively.

Tickle and Laugh

Probably, tickling is the oldest and safest way to stimulate laughter. Tickling and laughter are one of the first forms of communication between mother and baby. Laughter appears between three and a half to four months of life, long before he speaks. Thus, the mother uses the tickles to stimulate the baby's laughter and thus establish communication. Laughter in turn encourages the mother to continue to tickle, until there comes a time when the baby begins to complain, at which time the mother stops.

For the same fact that it is more difficult to laugh alone, it is also difficult for a person to tickle themselves. Tickling is an integral part of the game, so when you pet a person, you try to escape and laugh, but try to return them. In the process of giving and receiving tickles, there is a kind of neurological programming that causes people to establish links, and the same thing happens with sex. The armpits, the palms of hands and soles of the feet are areas whose stimulation by tickling laughter produces more easily.

Laughter Is Contagious

Like yawning, laughter is a neurologically programmed social behavior, whose origin lies in synchronizing the state of group behavior. Is, for example, why there is a hint of laughter in sitcoms on television? When we hear another person laugh at something, we immediately look at it and consider it more fun than if that person does not laugh, and then we smile or even laugh.

Laughter and Sex

Both men and women laugh to the same extent. However, the situation that produces the most laughter is when a man talks to a woman, or vice versa, and in this situation the woman is the one who leads the laughter and the man the leader of laughter production. As with speech, laughter of women generally presents more acute tone than that of men.  the a One

48

of the characteristics of the most attractive men for women is the sense of humor, although not precisely the ability to laugh. That is, the woman looks for a man who makes her laugh and does not laugh too much.

Laughter as a Mechanism for Controlling Others

The relationship between laughter and world events is modulated by culture and society. Currently, we relate laughter to the idea of "being happy and feeling good." However, Plato and Aristotle, among other authors who wrote about laughter, had a darker view of her. For example, they found public executions fun, something that is currently politically incorrect, just as they also laughed, in addition to the people in their group, people from other groups, such as other ethnicities or races. At present, our language nuances such a difference: laughing at someone is not the same as laughing at someone. For Robert Province, ridiculous laughter is an ancestral instinctive mechanism different from group laughter that served to modulate the behavior of individuals who did not belong to the group itself, for them to adapt and integrate into it. The anthropologist Verena Alberti uses the terms «laughter of welcome» and laughter of exclusion.

According to the scientist, that is the reason why people laugh in embarrassing or unpleasant circumstances. He affirms that laughter is an instrument to change the behavior of others. In an uncomfortable situation, such as a dispute, laughter represents a gesture of appeasement to lessen anger and tension. If the other person is infested, the risk of confrontation is dissipated.

Provine's observations suggested that social rank determines patterns of laughter, especially in the workplace; bosses easily provoke laughter from their subordinates and make jokes at their expense, telling that the phenomenon is generally a response to submission to the domain.

Laughter as the Origin of Language

According to Robert Provine, linguists and language scholars do not pay due attention to laughter. In contrast, physiology of the larynx and various parts of the vocal pathways does play a role in the production of sound. In his own words:

Laughter is a portion of the universal human vocabulary, and if we want to understand how the brain produces sound we should analyze behaviors that everyone has in the same way; that is, studying laughter - if we're going to understand human behavior - will be like using E. coli, or the fruit fly, to understand the mechanism of genetics. Instead of facing the immense complexity of nature, we try to concentrate on a small molecule, which is a part, which can be better accessed.-Robert Provine

Chapter 10: Mixed Signals

Understanding one another is a communication challenge that many people experience from time to time. One of the causes behind this is that everyone seems to see the world through their perspective. It is, after all, the only way that makes sense. Your experiences, your story, and your interactions form the guideline for your life and how you

assume everyone else should live their lives.

Because of this block perception, miscommunication happens more often than most people can admit. This explains why we jump to conclusions or make assumptions where we should not. The problem with mixed signals is that everyone ends up dealing with the aftermath of consuming false information. In most cases, people don't respond. They react, and it never ends well until they both realize it was all miscommunication from reading mixed signals.

Many relationships have suffered the curse of mixed signals, and since many people are afraid of being vulnerable, things can get murky very fast. Mixed signals are about inconsistency. They happen a lot in personal relationships, especially when someone's actions and words do not align, and the only thing consistent about them is the misalignment.

In some cases, mixed signals might be intentional and some accidental. Intended mixed signals include a situation where someone you like is not ready to commit to you because perhaps they are hoping that they can find someone better. An accidental scenario is when someone sends you a message, trying to express their feelings toward you, but the news does not come off the way they intended it.

Whichever reason behind mixed signals, they generate unnecessary stress and frustration. You might even start doubting yourself, wondering whether you are in the right place with the right person or whether you deserve to be there in the first place. When you are continually feeling unsure of your position, unaware of your role, you can start feeling insecure.

This is one of the challenges behind misreading people. When you meet someone and misread their body language and other communication cues, you can assume something about them when they don't feel the same way. Mixed signals are widespread in young relationships because you are unsure what you are getting into. You are not sure whether this is the right thing to do or whether they are the right person for you and so forth. There are many uncharted territories in new relationships, and as you are trying to learn more about each other, the risk of vulnerability is always high.

Why Mixed Signals Happen

Unless you were a target for specific reasons, very few people get into a relationship to mislead you. People tend to be genuine, or at least they try to be. One of the challenges they experience is poor communication. If you like each other, there is a fear of saying or doing the wrong thing. You want to be perfect in the eyes of this new person you like, and as a result, you create an environment where you are always walking on eggshells to impress them. Your intentions might be clear and genuine, but miscommunication breeds mixed signals.

So how does this happen? Well, first of all, many people don't know how to express their feelings. Relationships today are so complicated. One person might be in several relationships simultaneously, each of which is serving a different purpose in their lives. It gets worse when you are in a relationship without being fully aware that you are. This hinders your ability to express your true feelings to someone. Besides, what exactly are your true feelings? If you can't understand what you want, it is difficult for someone else to. Enter technology, and the swamp gets muddier.

We can hide so much behind our screens. You can exchange thousands of text messages with someone, throw in some emojis and memes to make it even juicier. Still, in reality, this only keeps you from opening up about your feelings and letting someone else know how vulnerable you are in their presence.

You don't get to experience body language in a text message. All you have is the text, which can be misunderstood and taken out of context. Without any other clues, it is not easy to decide over text messaging.

Instant messaging and communication today is something everyone enjoys. When you keep messaging someone all the time, it feels weird when they don't respond to you instantly. One of the worst and standard mixed signals today is "delayed response." People can read so much into silence. Perhaps you are intentionally ignoring them. Maybe you are no longer interested, perhaps you are with someone else, or perhaps you don't have your phone. Many thoughts occur when someone takes a radio silence approach, even when the situation was not in their control. Well, how else would you have known that, right? By the time you get back to them, all the thoughts that had crossed the sender's mind have them in a mood, which affects the nature of your communication.

Interpreting Popular Mixed Signals

The thing about mixed signals is that you have been a perpetrator or victim at one point in time. If you have been at either end of the spectrum, you can easily understand how frustrating it can be. How do you interpret the mixed signals? What do they mean for you or the person you are trying to communicate with? The following are some examples that might help:

When the Effort Fizzles Away. You might know this too well. You meet someone, and you can't seem to get enough time to spend together. However, a few days or weeks later, the effort to impress you is not there. It feels like they are not even trying. What happened? What changed? Are you not worth chasing after?

There are many possibilities behind this. One explanation is that the other person is struggling to keep up appearances. This happens when they set themselves up to fail. How does this happen? On the first meeting, someone portrays themselves as something else, someone else than who they truly are. Everything about the persona they introduce you to is fake.

However, soon after you have known each other for a while, they may feel they can now get back to being their true selves and live the life they are used to. The challenge here is that they leave you at a crossroads because, while you are worried, they might have changed because of something you did or lack, it is all about them.

Lukewarm Reactions and Responses. One moment, you are all having the time of your life, then suddenly, someone is distant and withdraws like you did something wrong. Sounds familiar? Well, Katy Perry says it better in "Hot n Cold."

It is challenging to deal with someone who operates like this. How can they sustain a very healthy and deep conversation that is so fulfilling and satisfying, then the next minute they are so empty you can fill them up with a gallon of water? Why can't someone make up their mind at once and let you in?

In this case, most people have their options open. You might think you are in the right place, but they are not. They are hoping something better comes along, and they will move on as soon as it does. Apart from those who keep their options open, you also might be dealing with someone who has an avoidant attachment method, which means they will pull away as soon as they feel something stable and reliable is about to happen in their lives. Whichever the case, interacting with such a person is not easy. It is frustrating because you will never be good enough for them. They cannot communicate what they want or how, and they would instead go about their lives oblivious to your suffering.

Communicating Without Mixed Signals

Mixed signals are frustrating for everyone—recipient and sender alike. The misunderstanding and misinterpretation can turn you into a villain when you meant well. Effective communication depends on the kind of response you get. To get the best and appropriate response, you must also ensure you don't send mixed signals.

Try to ensure your body language aligns with your words. Body language can throw someone off your vibe and distort the intended message completely. Pick your words wisely. Some words carry more weight than others in different situations. If you need to be assertive in a conversation, use emphatic words. Aggressive words will distort your communication.

If you are meeting someone, be keen on your posture. An assertive stance makes you more approachable. Relax and keep your head up. Speak in a warm, assuring tone, and try to vary your style through the sentences to make them assertive.

If you have to highlight a point, use the right gestures to help you. It would be best to encourage participation from other people around you too so that they feel they are part of the conversation and not just a passive audience.

Written communication can easily be confusing, especially since the recipient has no idea what was going through your mind. Try to eliminate any source of ambiguity in your writing. If you have to convey emotions, make them clear and precise. You can explain further where you feel you need to so that there is no doubt in the recipient's mind about what you mean.

Punctuation is another area where mixed signals are standard. Use the right punctuation marks. A comma in the wrong place can change the perceived meaning of a sentence to something else. Avoid using capital letters where they are not needed. Capital letters usually read like you are shouting at the reader (Rabern, 2015).

When communicating with someone over the phone, you must think your conversation through before you call them. Plan what you want to discuss with them ahead of time. This allows you sufficient time to get in the right frame of mind and not miss the point. Since you have had enough time to prepare for the call, listen to the recipient, and allow them enough time to convey their response.

In the same manner that you would convey your message to an audience, use tonal variation to stress the critical messages. Ensure the listener acknowledges the important parts of the message.

Always present yourself in your true form. This is one of the best ways you can avoid mixed signals. Authenticity is very difficult to fake. Do not change your mannerisms because you want to impress someone. Be who you are. Be genuine so that if someone reads and interacts with you, they are not conflicted in the person they are dealing with. It also helps because you will be interacting with their genuine reactions and responses.

It is important to hold everyone accountable for inappropriate communication skills, including yourself. Try to encourage everyone around you to be clear in the way they address issues. If you don't do this and instead allow the communication to prevail, you create an environment where people's mixed signals are okay.

Chapter 11: Can I Learn How to Fake My Body Language?

The next thing that we need to take a look at is how to fake your body language. Some people feel that manufacturing this kind of thing is impossible. They know that it is hard to hide many of the body signs that you are trying to show to others. This doesn't mean that the process is impossible to work with, but it takes a lot of time and effort.

Many people are not aware of the different body language and

nonverbal language cues they send to the world. But this doesn't mean that you are not able to fake some of it, and get others to think that you feel and act in a certain way. Keep in mind here that doing this is going to be difficult sometimes. It is not always as easy as it seems, and you have to be constantly aware of what you are doing. If you forget to do this and aren't paying attention to the different parts of your body language and how they are working together, you will find that some part of you will betray you, and you will lose the trust in the person you are trying to work with.

The good news here is that with a little bit of practice and some hard thinking at the same time, you can control the various aspects of your personality and figure out how to make people see different things with your body language. Some of the things that you should focus on include:

The Eye Contact

The first thing that we are going to focus on when we need to fake our body language is eye contact. You need to make sure that your eye contact is on point. This is one of the easiest things to fake, and if you are messing up with this still in your personal and professional life, then it means that you are going to have to work on that before you get a chance to work with some of the others.

Think about the last time you talked with someone who was not able to maintain eye contact. Whether it was them focusing down all of the time, looking at their phone or their watch, or even glancing towards the door all of the time, it felt like they wanted to look anywhere but at you. Eventually, it made you feel like you were not necessary, and you tried to stop the conversation and move on, no matter how important the information was.

Don't be a person like this. You don't want to make the other person feel like they are not necessary. You want them to know that you are interested in them, that what they have to say is worth your attention. And the best way to do this is to make sure that your eye contact is good.

There is a nice balance here. You do not want your gaze to be so intense that you make the other person feel uncomfortable. We all know this kind of look. It includes no blinking and may feel like you are trying to stare down with the other person. Focus on a gaze that shows that you are interested, but include some blinking and some emotion in them.

Your Arm Movements

Pay attention to the arm movements that you are doing. If you want to show another person that you are excited and happy about something, it probably is not a good idea to stand with the arms crossed. Happiness and excitement are going to include a lot of arm movements going all of the time. The bigger the movements (within reason, don't try to hit the other person with the flailing arms), the more animated you will appear to others.

However, if you want to appear like you are calm and collected, or like you are more withdrawn (there may be times when you want someone to leave you alone for example), then crossing your arms, or at least keeping the arms and hands close to the body, maybe the right option for your needs.

So, when you are trying to fake your arm movements as a part of the body language, the best way to do this is to figure out what mood you want to portray to the other person. If you're going to show that you are animated and excited, then the arm movements need to be away from the body and nice and big. If you're going to show that you are more withdrawn, then the arms and hands need to be close to the body.

The Smile

It is essential to spend some time focusing on the smile that you give off. Many of us have been trained on how to give a fake smile in any situation, but there is a big difference between the phony smile and a genuine smile. You may be able to fake it with some people, but you often need to try and get a real and genuine smile on your face to impress those around you.

Remember that with a genuine smile, you need to use more than the sides of the mouth. This one includes the whole face and even some crinkles around the eyes. This can be done even when faking it, but you need to do some practice. An excellent way to do this is to spend some time in a mirror, work on the smile, and try to get the whole face into it.

Doing a smile in front of the mirror is going to make a big difference. You can look at how the smile will appear to others, and get a general feel of how it will feel to do this. Then, when you are in front of someone else using this smile, you will know how to make this smile appear for you without the mirror present.

Your Stance

The last thing that we are going to look at is your stance. You need to make sure that you are picking out the right kind of view to impress another person and let them know that you are interested. Of course, the posture is going to be an essential part of all of this. You want to stand upright, rather than to slouch, and you want to make sure that you show off the confidence inside you.

There is more to this one than just the posture that you use, though. If you can add a few more things into this, you will find out that it will help you get some results with how comfortable others are around you. The first thing to look at is your feet. If you want the other person to think that you are interested in them and that your whole attention is on them, make sure the feet are pointed in the right direction. They need to be pointed at the person you are talking to, rather than to the side or even worse, towards the door.

The way that you lean is important as well. If your posture has you leaning towards the door, or at all away from the other person, then this is going to give them the thought that you are not interested in them at all. But, leaning slightly towards them, with your body leaning in, shows that you are interested in what they are saying to them.

It is hard to fake the body language that you are doing with another person. While we often wish to show off a certain kind of appearance to others, it will be tough to do this. You have to be careful about how you do this. But with some practice and tips, you will become more aware of the different cues that our bodies are giving off to others, and it is a lot easier for you to give off the appearance that you would like.

Chapter 12: How to Have a Positive Effect on Others

Part of coming across as respectable to other people and getting along with them is projecting confidence and positivity. Someone who is seen as a positive person will have a much easier time connecting to a wider range of people and enjoying better opportunities in life, due to their approachable nature. This makes it highly important to learn how to come across this way.

How to Have a Positive Effect on Others

It's not as hard as it seems to become a positive influence for those people around you, and you can start right now. Here are some simple actions that can have a positive effect on others:

- Approachable Facial Expressions: A genuine smile tells the other person you are warm, confident and approachable. This build trusts.

- Subtle Mirroring: Match the other person's movements subtly. This helps build rapport through establishing a common ground. It also shows your similarities as you mimic others. People will naturally observe this even if they aren't aware of it on the surface, and will instantly like you more.

- Nodding: Nodding while someone is talking shows you are engaged and listening. Many people are used to people being distracted while they are talking, so this is a simple way to show you care and are truly hearing the other person and listening.

Also, you can nod while you are talking to help influence the person to agree with you. It is no guarantee, but when you nod while asking a question, people often unknowingly nod as well, signifying that they agree with what you are saying.

- Don't Sit Down: Standing up helps you feel powerful and confident. This is useful when giving presentations. Just make sure not to stand over anyone, as that is a sign of a threat to most people.

- Be Mindful of your Head Position: Tilting your head or body toward someone shows you are interested. If you make others feel important then you have the opportunity to influence them positively.

- Pointing your Feet: The way your feet point says a lot about whether you want to be where you are. Much like head positioning, the position of your feet can also have a subconscious effect on someone. Pointing your feet towards someone shows you are interested. It is a positive signal that builds trust. On the other hand, pointing your feet away shows that you subconsciously are waiting for a chance to escape as soon as possible.

What Can Mastering Body Language Do for You?

It's possible to improve your life and interpersonal interactions greatly by becoming mindful of your nonverbal cues. Research shows that having correct nonverbal language will aid you in the following ways:

- Less Misunderstandings: This can help connect with others, meaning that you are less likely to be misunderstood. Since misunderstandings are at the base of most negative interactions and resentment, this is a must.

- Better Performance: The right posture will help you with your performance, since it directly impacts how you come across and your mood. Utilizing "power postures" will help you feel more confident. You can also embody the idea of determination in your posture to make yourself feel stronger and more confident.

- Small shifts in your nonverbal cues can have a great effect on your existence, overall. Here are some specific ways that this can happen for you.

- A Posture of Power: Our body language has a direct role in the people we are, whether we're aware of it. This simple factor directly shapes our personalities, abilities, power, and confidence levels. Not only does the way you carry yourself send others a clear message about you, but it sends your brain a clear message, as well, and impacts the way you act and feel.

Our animal relatives show their dominance and power by making themselves larger, expanding, taking up more room, and stretching their bodies out. In other words, establishing power is all about opening your body up, and people do this as well. If you are feeling nervous, small, or incapable, simply open your body up and pay attention to your mood shifts. You should feel suddenly much more capable and self-assured.

For example, you might wish you feel more confident or powerful in situations where you are interviewing for a job and wish to showcase your abilities and assertiveness. You might also wish to show that you're confident in a classroom situation or a leadership position. As you walk into a negotiation, you would want to send a message that you know what you want and are well-aware of your abilities.

For situations like this, or any others you need a confidence boost in, you can stand erect, with your shoulders pushed back, your stance wide, and your head upward. Raise your arms to make a "Y" as in the YMCA dance, and you will instantly feel more powerful and energetic. What is it about this posture that helps us feel better and more confident? It affects our hormones, resulting in a couple of key ingredients in the feeling of dominance. These are cortisol (the hormone of stress) and testosterone (the hormone of dominance).

Males in high, alpha positions of power in groups of primates have low levels of cortisol and high levels of testosterone, but this isn't just primates. Effective and powerful people in leadership positions have the same pattern, meaning that they are assertive and powerful, but don't react strongly to stress. Even in tough situations, they can stay calm and handle business effectively. Research shows that adopting the power position we just told you about for a minimum of a couple minutes will lower your cortisol levels while boosting testosterone. In other words, you will be priming your brain to deal with whatever situations might pop up during the day.

More Postures for Improving Your Levels of Performance:

The posture of our body directly influences our mind, which results in our specific behaviors and actions. This means that if we can convince our physical bodies to lead our minds to more positive places, our performance will skyrocket. Here are some postures that are recommended by professionals for positive results.

• Tensing up for Willpower: If you're in a situation that calls for more willpower, you should tense your muscles. This posture shows your body that you're tensed and ready for anything, no matter what. This will send the message to your brain that resilience is needed on a mental level.

• Hand Gestures for Persuasion: If you're in a position where you need to persuade other people in conversation, make sure you utilize gestures of the hands. This shows that you believe in what you're saying and also helps you come across as more convincing. Others will feel more positive about you if you do this.

• Cross your Arms for Persistence: Having crossed arms can mean that you're closed off, which is bad in certain circumstances. In others, however, this is a useful frame of mind. For example, you might be in a situation where stubbornness is a good quality and you need it to stay persistent. This is a good time to cross your arms.

How to Gain the Advantage in Body Language:

Body language is a whole new world that can change your life. When it comes to any situation that handles interactions with others, it's a must for being successful. Here are some tips for getting ahead in this area.

- Raising the Eyebrows: When someone is out in public and sees someone they know, their eyebrows will move up automatically, just a tiny bit. No matter what culture, this response is present. The good news here is that you can start using this to your benefit anytime you meet a new person. Try to do it in the first few seconds that you're talking to them. Raising your eyebrows just a bit will make you appear more approachable and friendly, creating a positive connection between you and the other person.

- Remember Times you were Enthusiastic: Having charisma just means that you have enthusiasm and that it shows clearly to other people. This means that wanting to look charismatic to others requires simply appearing enthusiastic. To do this at will, simply call to your mind another time that made you feel enthusiastic. Once you re recalling this past event that made you very excited and enthusiastic, this will come across in your nonverbal cues, showing that you're charismatic and confident. This is a contagious effect and others will feel more positive from noticing your enthusiasm and charisma.

- Smile for more Resilience: If you're faced with a hard task, you can make it feel easier to yourself by smiling. The body's natural reaction to reaching exhaustion is making a pained grimace. However, experiments have shown that smiling increases your ability to press on and keep going through that feeling. Athletes were shown to be able to do a few more reps if they started smiling during their performance.

Grimacing sends your brain the message that you aren't able to continue doing what you're doing. Your brain then reacts to that by pumping you feel of stress chemicals, adding to your exhaustion and difficulty. Smiling, on the other hand, shows your brain that you can keep going, resulting in a better performance and more resilience.

Using these cues will help you a lot with your general positivity and how others perceive it. Shifting your nonverbal cues and body language will influence how those around you perceive you and how you see yourself. On top of this, your facial expressions and postures are always sending your brain messages which then influence the hormones your body is releasing. This is a great power to have if you're aware of it and use it in the right way, but not being aware of it can have negative results and effects, not only on yourself but also on others. Take the power into your own hands and become more positive by using this connection.

Chapter 13: Confidence and How It Is Displayed

Confidence is a very powerful emotion in today's society. An individual who appears very confident can go to a very far places. By appearing confident, a person can attract suitable mates and be given promotions based on their perceived leadership skills. Because of this, confidence is very commonly displayed in different ways. However, confidence is also faked a lot of times to get ahead in life. We will go through the common ways that confidence is displayed through body language. Besides, we will also go through how you can spot a lack of confidence in an individual.

Displaying Confidence

· Posture

Posture is very important in the appearance of confidence. An individual's posture can say a lot about their perceived level of confidence. Confident posture is defined by legs lined with the individual's shoulders and feet approximately four to six inches apart. Weight is typically distributed equally on both legs, and shoulders are pushed back slightly. A straight back is also very typical of someone with extreme confidence. Individuals with this sort of posture are considered assertive and tend to project confidence. This is because an individual with this posture is seen as being able to "stand tall" regardless of their height and are also perceived as being very open to those talking to them, as they are unafraid of any attacks or criticism.

· Hands

Hands are very important in trying to appear confident. It is important to remember when trying to display confidence through your hands to keep them calm and still. Rapidly moving one's hands is a sign of nervousness or anxiety.

· Eye Contact

Having the ability to maintain long and strong eye contact with another is a good sign that an individual feels confident. This is because showing eye contact with another person is a very vulnerable feeling and position. This is because our eyes can show a lot about how we feel in a situation. By maintaining good eye contact, we show the other person that we are unafraid of what they may see within our eyes. This is a sign of extreme confidence, as it shows that you are self-assured in your feelings and believes that you are unafraid of how a person will interpret what they see in your eyes.

· Mirroring Body Language

Mirroring the body language of those around us elicits a sort  of understanding and seeks acceptance from those around us. This raises our confidence level as we humans strive to be liked by those around us. Because those around us will subconsciously begin to like us more by mirroring their body language, they will also be confident because of their positive view.

· Fidgeting

It is very important to remember not to fidget when you are trying to display levels of confidence. Fidgeting in any form—no matter what part of your body is doing the movement—shows signs of nervousness and anxiety. In addition to this, it can simply annoy those around us. People are often irritated by constant rhythmic tapping or brushing noises. This is something to keep in mind if you are an individual who likes to bounce their leg or tap their foot at simple moments.

Ways to Spot a Lack of Confidence in a Person

· A very common sign of lack of confidence in an individual is if they are constantly touching their phone while in social situations or while alone. If an individual finds themselves unable to sit still during a social situation where they don't know very many people, this may be a sign that they lack confidence. Checking their phone is a sign that they feel uncomfortable in a social situation and cannot connect with those around them.

· Another sign of a lack of confidence in an individual is a quick backing down during a disagreement to avoid arguing with another person. An individual with an extreme lack of confidence will not want to cause problems with a person that they disagree with. Because of this, they often negotiate their views to avoid conflict. This shows that people lack confidence because they are not assured in their own opinions and would rather back down than express themselves honestly.

· Another common sign of a lack of confidence in an individual is their inability to leave their homes without makeup or hairstyling. This is a very obvious sign of a lack of confidence because it shows that individuals don't feel that they are worth being looked at unless they have something on their bodies or face to make them look more beautiful. Putting makeup on or doing their hair gives a false sense of self-esteem to an individual, which people with low self-esteem or confidence rely on very heavily?

· An individual with low confidence will also tend to take constructive criticism far too personally. If a person gives this individual constructive criticism about something, they will take it way too seriously and end up feeling very strong negative emotions. This is a huge sign of low confidence and low self-esteem because this individual is not emotionally balanced enough to handle constructive criticism from those around them.

· Individuals who have low confidence or self-esteem will also find themselves afraid to contribute their opinion in a conversation. They will often second-guess themselves before they say anything instead of diving into an interesting conversation. They may find themselves stuttering or putting themselves down. This is because these individuals don't know how well their opinions will be received and are afraid of others taking their opinions negatively. This is a sign of low confidence or self-esteem because they care very deeply about how the people they make contact with view them.

· An individual who has difficulty with confidence also find themselves extremely indecisive with very simple and basic decisions. They may change their minds very often after coming to a decision. This is a sign of low self-confidence because this individual cannot trust their own opinions or decisions. This is especially a sign of low self-confidence when this applies to very simple tasks or simple decisions.

· Individuals with low self-confidence will also have extreme difficulty handling genuine compliments from those around them. They tend not to think that they are worthy of such good compliment, and they usually put them down or not accept them.

· Individuals struggling with low self-confidence will also tend to give up very soon with things that they are trying to do or achieve. They may have goals and dreams that they want to accomplish but will give up before they begin. This is a sign of low self-confidence because they do not believe that they can accomplish these goals and dreams before they even start.

· Individuals that struggle with low self-confidence will also tend to compare themselves with those around them. They tend to have very strong attention to the people who are doing better than them and will point out all of the ways they are not doing and those around them. This is a strong sign of low self-confidence because it says that the person in question does not view themselves as very successful or doing very well.

· Slouching is a very common display of low self-confidence in an individual. Why so? It is because lowering the center of a person's body is a sign that a person is unwilling to hold up the weight of their upper body themselves. It sends off a signal that that individual is not proud of himself/herself. Because of these things, this is a big sign of low self-confidence.

To detect low self-confidence in an individual, all you have to do is look out for some of these common signs of low self-esteem and self-confidence. You can also detect low self-confidence or low self-esteem within yourself by looking out for these common signs. If you find that you or someone you know has low self-esteem or confidence, you can begin to work on them by saying very positive statements about yourself regularly.